Lighthouses

A Guide to Many of Maine's Coastal and Offshore Guardians

Text by Barbara Feller-Roth

Conceived and developed
by DeLorme Mapping Company

Freeport, Maine 04032
ISBN 0-89933-050-9

Table of Contents

Cover Photo by Charles Hobart

INTRODUCTION

Lighthouses have evolved from rudimentary bonfires on a high point of land or a kettle of burning tar at the top of a pole to beacons of beveled glass gracing handsome granite towers. The transition has taken 200 years. It was initiated in New England by an increasing number of shipwrecks among the burgeoning commerce of this young country. As shipping increased, the number of lighthouses multiplied.

Unfortunately, the quality and management of the early lighthouses suffered from the rapid growth. A Lighthouse Board was created by Congress in 1852 to inspect and upgrade every lighthouse in the country. In 1910 the Board was replaced by the Bureau of Lighthouses, under whose jurisdiction the U.S. Lighthouse Service became the largest organization of its kind in the world. The last change in command came in 1939, when the U.S. Coast Guard absorbed the Lighthouse Service. The tradeoff for civilian lighthouse keepers and their families keeping their lonely vigil at remote outposts was a string of updated lighthouses and beacons that are eminently reliable.

With its long ragged coast and shoaly waters, Maine has more lighthouses and beacons than any other state its size. In 1980, there were 71 lighthouses between Boon Island off York and West Quoddy Head in Lubec. About seven are still attended, either as stag lights, with several men attending exposed locations, or family lights, with one or more families living in the refurbished keeper's dwellings, such as Portland Head Light or Burnt Island off Boothbay Harbor. Attended lights welcome visitors to the grounds, although climbing into the light towers is arranged on an individual basis, usually by calling ahead.

At the stag lights offshore, Coast Guardsmen are on duty for one to four weeks at a time and are transported to and from the mainland by buoy tenders or, in winter, helicopters. They send out weather information and radio beacons for boats to orient themselves and monitor the light.

To provide a recognizable aid to navigation no two beacons in a given area have the same characteristics, so that the interval of flash or the color of the light (white, red or green)—which are indicated on navigational charts—are different at neighboring lighthouses. Before lights were electrified, they were flashed by a weight-actuated lens drive, a cuckoo clock-like mechanism that rotated panels in front of the light at fixed intervals. Electrified lights also blink at fixed intervals and today are called either flashing or occulting; in the latter the period of light is always longer than the period of darkness, as opposed to flashing, where the period of light is always less than the period of darkness. Another variety of navigational aid is a daymark, which has no electrified beacon and is visible only during daylight.

Lighthouse technology improved immensely after 1822, when the French scientist Augustin Fresnel perfected prisms, refracting lenses and a powerful magnifying glass to concentrate the beacon. The flame from a single oil burner that was intensified by a Fresnel lens could be seen for miles.

Many of Maine's older lighthouses have been automated with modern beacons or preserved as historic monuments. Due to economic considerations, the Coast Guard is planning to automate almost all lighthouses in the near future. The days will be gone of colorful lighthouse keepers and their lonely, dramatic and daring lives.

Boon Island Light — York

Boon Island Light, Mount Desert Rock Light and Saddleback Ledge Light off Vinalhaven have the dubious distinction of being located on rock ledges so devoid of soil that lighthouse keepers stationed there hauled earth from the mainland to grow flowers and vegetables. By late fall every year, however, the soil had been washed away by the fierce storms that swept these remote outposts.

Boon Island Light was built in 1811 atop massive granite boulders hewn on the mainland and ferried to Boon Island to augment the ledge. The storms at this location have carried these stones, each weighing several tons, from one shore of the island to the other. And heavy seas repeatedly delayed the construction of the first lighthouse, a 50-foot-high wooden tower, because workmen were unable to land their craft. The jagged ledge was notorious for ripping the hulls of vessels that approached it.

Five years after it was built, the original wooden tower was washed away in a storm and a stone tower was erected in its place. Its construction was marred by the drowning of three workmen whose boat capsized in heavy seas. That tower, the site's first attended lighthouse, was also swept away in a storm and in 1855 it was replaced by the 133-foot granite tower that still stands.

Boon Island is one of the state's most dangerous and isolated stations, about 6.5 miles from the nearest headland and nine miles from York, its former mail and supply base. It was a long row or sail for the keepers to renew their stores. Because winter storms often confined them to the island for months on end, the keepers stocked up in the fall with sufficient supplies and food to carry them through until spring. In her poem *The Watch of Boon Island*, Celia Thaxter, daughter of one-time keeper at the neighboring Isles of Shoals Light, captured the lonely vigil of such folk among the wild waves and fierce storms. Yet one keeper, William W. Williams, spent 27 years on Boon Island and holds the record for service at that light. In the late 1800s, however, Boon Island was made a stag station because it was considered too dangerous for women and children.

Characteristics and Location

Boon Island Light is a conical gray granite tower connected to a dwelling, 137 feet from mean high water, and 133 feet from the ground to the center of the beacon. It is a group occulting white light flashing every 30 seconds, visible for 18 miles.

Photo Courtesy of Maine Publicity Bureau

Cape Neddick Light — York

Cape Neddick Light, popularly known as the Nubble, is one of the most photographed, illustrated and readily identifiable lighthouses on the eastern seaboard. Built in 1879, the original tower still stands.

The narrow channel that separates the Nubble from the mainland has been negotiated at low tide by lighthouse keepers in hip boots. At other times, a dory is used to ferry family members, such as children attending school on the mainland. In 1912, an enterprising lighthouse keeper, William Brooks, ferried visitors to the Nubble for ten cents a head, and accommodated up to 300 people a day. He encouraged visitors by supplying fishing poles, lines and bait. Unfortunately, his sideline interfered with his lighthouse duties. When his moonlighting was discovered, he was forced to resign. Brooks' tombstone is in a Kittery Point graveyard.

In 1919, Lucy Glidden Burke, the daughter of lighthouse keeper Captain James Burke, wrote about their lifestyle—keeping the buildings scrupulously clean for monthly inspections and anticipating the arrival of government ships twice a year with oil and supplies, such as 100-pound sacks of beans and large stores of staples like sugar, flour and molasses. The food supply was well supplemented by fresh eggs and milk from the family chickens and cow, and by ducks and lobsters, crabs, mussels and fish caught by the lighthouse keeper. Rainwater was funneled from the roof of the keeper's house to a cistern in the basement and hand pumps raised it to the kitchen. Indoor plumbing and electricity did not come until 1938. The old-style fog bell also needed tending: when it was in constant use, the 32-inch cast iron wheel had to be wound every four hours, and it took 20 minutes of hard winding to do the job.

Entertainment came from a pump organ in the living room. Unpleasant chores came during every fall migration, when hundreds of birds flew against the tower at night, attracted by the beacon. They had to be raked from the rocks below the following morning

By Lucy Burke's account, the family ate well and enjoyed their accessibility to the mainland. Her father took this post, after spending more than 25 years at the more isolated lights at Boon Island and White Island in the Isles of Shoals, so Lucy could attend school on the mainland. She and her school friends were carried piggy back across the sandbar on her father's shoulders at low tide or rowed across in the dory at high water.

Because of its relative accessibility, the Nubble has had scores of visitors. Records from 1930 report more than 1000 visitors from 11 countries and 32 states. Part of the attraction, at least between 1930 and 1943, was the 19-pound cat owned by the last of the Lighthouse Service keepers Eugene Colman. Known as the best mouser in Maine, the cat swam the channel three or four times a day and was a great lure for summer visitors.

The Coast Guard assumed full administration of lighthouses in 1939. Until its automation in 1987, the Nubble had always been attended and maintained as a family light. The daughter of one keeper was married inside the lantern around the turn of the century, and a child was born at the station in the early 1900s.

The history of illumination at the Nubble includes a progression from whale oil, until it became too expensive; lard oil; colza; kerosene and incandescent oil vapor lamp with a mantle similar to a Coleman lamp, in the late 1800s; and electricity, in 1938. Colza was an experimental oil derived from cabbages, with a subsidy paid to farmers as an incentive to grow the crop for this purpose. A variety of oils was tried in an effort to find one that could withstand the extreme temperatures of exposed locations. Winter winds of more than 100 miles per hour have been recorded at the Nubble. The current illumination is a 1000-watt bulb inside a plastic lens which replaced a fourth order Fresnel lens when the lighthouse was automated in 1987. Fourth order lenses are the most common on the Maine coast; only one first order lens, the largest of the lenses, is found in Maine, at Seguin Island at the mouth of the Kennebec River.

The popularity of the Nubble, and the sentiment stirred by it, were illustrated recently when the Coast Guard, as part of routine maintenance, painted the old brick oil house white, to match the rest of the buildings on the island. More than 1000 telephone calls to the South Portland Coast Guard Station protested the change, and the oil house was restored to its former color—red.

Characteristics and Location

Cape Neddick Light, a white conical tower with a dwelling and several outbuildings, is 88 feet from mean high water, and 41 feet from the ground to the center of the beacon—an equal interval red flash every six seconds, visible for 13 miles and accompanied by a foghorn.

The lighthouse is just offshore from Cape Neddick, at the end of Nubble Road, about 1.1 miles off Route 1A at the end of York Beach. Although traversing the sandbar across the channel to the lighthouse is not encouraged, the structure is in fine view from the rocks on either side of the small parking area. The rocks are fun to climb, and fishermen, artists and photographers are almost always seen there. At high tide, lobster boats often ply the narrow channel. Seasonal lighthouse cruises out of Ogunquit also pass the Nubble (207-646-9476).

Photo by P.R. Hornby

Wood Island Light — Biddeford

Shipwrecks and murders have haunted the history of Wood Island Light since it was built near the mouth of the Saco River in 1808. Legend has it that the island has been jinxed since 1896 when a resident lobsterman killed the deputy sheriff and then committed suicide. It is believed that the site has been haunted ever since by the ghost of the murdered man.

Prior to 1869, Wood Island was forested. In that year, a terrific winter gale mowed down a broad swath of trees and a sweeping fire finished off those remaining.

Wood Island was the home of another famous lighthouse keeper's dog. Sailer was trained to ring the island's fog bell by tugging at the clapper cord with his teeth every time he heard a ship's bell near the lighthouse. The dog belonged to keeper Thomas Henry Orcutt in the 1850s.

Characteristics and Location

Formerly a family light, Wood Island Light was automated in 1986. It is a white conical granite tower connected to a dwelling at the east end of the island, at the entrance to Wood Island Harbor off Biddeford Pool. The tower is 71 feet from mean high water to the center of the beacon—alternating white and green lights every 10 seconds, visible for 16 and 14 miles, respectively. The station also has a foghorn.

Photo by Nance Trueworthy

Cape Elizabeth Light — Cape Elizabeth

Originally called Two Lights and located in what is now known as Two Lights State Park, Cape Elizabeth Light was built with two stone towers, one with a flashing light and one with a fixed beacon. The site was regarded as one of the most important on the East Coast, as it was south of the entrance to Portland Harbor, the state's largest port. The necessity of a strong beacon there was underlined after the sloop *Resolution* ran aground on ledges that had previously been marked only by a 45-foot-high rubblestone monument painted black and white. The old monument, built in 1811, was removed and two cast iron towers, 300 yards apart and 129 feet above mean high water, were built in 1829. Elisha Jordan was the first keeper; his annual salary was $450 and he stayed six years. His successors weathered the worst storm of the 19th century, the January sleet storm of 1876 that broke the glass and sash bars in every north window of the keeper's dwelling.

Much public outcry accompanied every attempt to dismantle one of Cape Elizabeth's beacons. Mariners favored them because as the only twin lights along that portion of the coast, they gave certainty to a ship's bearing. In 1855, when the west light was ordered discontinued and the east light converted, the protest was so great that the twin lights were retained. In 1924, however, the government ordered all twin lights in the country converted to single beacons and the west tower at Cape Elizabeth Light had its top dismantled. The east tower still stands. Matinicus Rock, the only other twin light in Maine, was also converted at the same time. The single beacon atop Cape Elizabeth Light is now four million candlepower, the most powerful of its kind on the New England Coast. It is still popularly referred to, however, as Two Lights.

Characteristics and Location

Cape Elizabeth Light is a white conical tower 67 feet from the ground to the middle of the beacon, a group flashing white light every 30 seconds, visible for 27 miles. The station also has a foghorn. The light has been automated and the keeper's dwelling is now privately owned.

The lighthouse, in Two Lights State Park off Route 77 in Cape Elizabeth, is easily accessible by car. The 41-acre park, open from April 15 to November, has a picnic area, trails and fishing from the ledges.

Portland Head Light — Cape Elizabeth

Portland Head Light is the oldest lighthouse in Maine. It was erected under George Washington's administration in 1791 at the entrance to the state's largest port, after the owners of 74 vessels in the Portland environs petitioned for a lighthouse. Because of the tenuous economy of the young country, the early structure was built of rubblestone instead of granite. Field stones no heavier than two men could hoist were gathered from nearby fields and hauled to the site by oxen. The stones were set in lime from limestone quarried in Rockland.

The lighthouse has had several major renovations over the years, including a new pyramidal bell tower with a 2000-pound bell built in 1869, when the great September storm swept away the old cast iron fog bell and caused the loss of at least 20 vessels. As late as 1962 tremendous waves cracked three walls of the engine house and the April 3, 1975 storm battered the wall of the whistle house, knocked out the fog horn and temporarily extinguished the beacon.

Henry Wadsworth Longfellow immortalized Portland Head Light in many lines composed while sitting

Photo by Alan Stevens

in his favorite spot on the promontory near the base of the tower. The poet frequently visited the popular keeper Captain Joshua Strout, who came to Portland Head in 1867 and served for more than 50 years.

Characteristics and Location

Portland Head Light has a white conical tower and connected dwelling. It is 101 feet from mean high water, and 80 feet from the ground to the center of the beacon—a flashing white light every 3.7 seconds, visible for 22 miles. The station also has a foghorn. From the tower's hurricane deck, on the southwest side of the entrance to Portland Harbor, can be seen more than 200 islands in the sweep of Casco Bay from Cape Elizabeth to Small Point. On a clear night, twelve lighted beacons are visible.

Portland Head is one of the most visited lights on the Atlantic seaboard. While scheduled for automation in 1990, it is currently a family light (207-799-2661) accessible by land, on the Shore Road in Cape Elizabeth, adjoining Fort Williams, formerly a major Army installation dating from before the Spanish-American War. The complex is open year-round, including holidays, from 8 am to 4 pm.

Ram Island Ledge Light — Portland

The most recent lighthouse to be built in Casco Bay is the Ram Island Ledge Light, erected in 1905 on a quarter-mile-long jagged finger of rock at the entrance to Portland Harbor. The new granite tower replaced a less obvious tripod beacon because the ledge presented such a great danger to shipping.

Because Ram Island Ledge is submerged at most tides, construction of the light tower took considerable time. The first granite blocks were cut in quarries on Vinalhaven and arrived in Portland in July 1903. When work was suspended for the winter at the end of September, the cisterns had been built, half the courses of block had been set and the tower was 32 feet high. Between April and November of the following year, the tower was completed and the illuminating devices were installed. In August, 1905, the beacon was lit and the fog bell was placed in operation.

Aficionados of lighthouses may note that the Ram Island Ledge Light looks almost identical to the Graves Light, outside Boston Harbor. They were built about the same time on almost equally exposed ledges.

Characteristics and Location

Ram Island Ledge Light is a light gray conical granite tower at the north side of the entrance to Portland Harbor. The tower is 77 feet from mean high water to the center of the beacon—a group flashing white light, flashing two seconds, then dark for three seconds, visible for 12 miles. The station also has a foghorn. The light was converted from kerosene to electricity in 1958. It has been unattended since 1959.

In the early 1900s, the ledge attracted picnickers and sea moss rakers since at low water about an acre of rock is high and dry. Currently, Casco Bay Lines ferries pass Ram Island Ledge Light on their way to the outer islands (207-774-7871).

Spring Point Ledge Light — South Portland

It took requests by seven steamship companies regularly serving Portland to bring a lighthouse and fog signal to Spring Point Ledge in 1897. Prior to that time, many ships had stranded on the partially submerged ledge.

The original lighthouse had a circular iron staircase connecting the first level (a cellar with coal compartments), the second level (the kitchen), the third level (the home and office of the head keeper) and the fourth level (the assistant keeper's quarters). From

Photo by Bernie Reim

there up was an iron ladder to the watch room (with the clock weight and bell striking mechanism) and the lantern room, with its heavy beveled glass lens. In 1934, the kerosene powered light was replaced by electricity.

Even at low tide, Spring Point Ledge Light is surrounded by water, so landing at the tower was originally accomplished with a tender raised on pulleys that were suspended from the catwalk. Exercise was limited to the circular staircase and the catwalk. It was said that 56 times around the tower's main deck constituted a one-mile jog.

The light was automated in 1934, and in 1951 a 900-foot-long breakwater was built from the shore to the light along the course of the ledge. The granite for the breakwater—50,000 tons of it—came from quarries in Biddeford and Wells.

Characteristics and Location

Spring Point Ledge Light is a white conical tower on a black cylindrical pier on the west side of the main channel into Portland Harbor. The tower is 54 feet from mean high water to the center of the beacon—a flashing white light every six seconds with two red sectors, visible for 14 miles (white) and 11 miles (red). The station also has a foghorn.

The lighthouse, located in the old Fort Preble area in South Portland, is accessible by land. It is also visible from Casco Bay Lines cruises to the outer islands (207-774-7871).

Halfway Rock Light — Portland

Named for its location about midway between Cape Elizabeth and Small Point, the west and east extremities of Casco Bay, Halfway Rock is a windswept bare ledge of about three acres surrounded by treacherous shoals. Except for a single landing site on the north shore, the ledge would be virtually inaccessible in all but calm seas.

Directly in the path of vessels that regularly ran up and down the coast, Halfway Rock was a menace to navigation. After several vessels were pounded to pieces on the ledge, a lighthouse was built, with massive granite blocks quarried on Chebeague Island in Casco Bay and cut at Fort Scammel in Portland Harbor. The light's completion had been delayed about a year by the difficulty of workmen landing on the ledge in all but summer and early fall, and by a hitch in a public works appropriation law. The lighthouse was finally completed in 1871, and its early keepers were relied on by the city of Portland to report the approach of vessels into the harbor.

Among the improvements over the years were a foghorn which in 1905 replaced the 1000-pound bell, and a progression from lard oil lamps to mineral oil—in 1883—and finally to electricity. In 1960, a modern dwelling was attached to the tower for the lighthouse keepers, whose duty was rotated among three men.

A South Portland buoy tender which brought supplies to the island once a week transported the keepers to and from the mainland. That was quite a change from the 11-mile row or sail into Portland made in small craft by keepers of the previous century.

But the fury of the sea affects even the modern installation. In October 1962, a storm that swamped the entire station ripped away half a 40-square-foot concrete helicopter landing pad and twisted catwalks and iron railings like twine.

Steamboats regularly plied the oft frequented shipping lane that was interrupted by Halfway Rock, and one potentially tragic incident occurred within sight of it. In an early morning fog on June 8,1906, the steamships *City of Rockland* and *City of Bangor,* both owned by the Eastern Steamship Company, and on the Boston to Bangor route, glanced off one another in a last minute maneuver to avoid a head-on collision. Five staterooms on the *Rockland* were crushed and the stem of the *Bangor* was destroyed to the waterline. The *Rockland* was able to continue, but the *Bangor* had to seek repairs in Portland Harbor.

Characteristics and Location

Halfway Rock Light is a white granite tower with attached dwelling 76 feet from mean high water to the center of the beacon—a flashing red light every five seconds and visible for 19 miles. The light is about 11 miles off the coast at Portland, and while day sailors from Casco Bay frequently make the vicinity of the rock their midday destination, landing on the ragged shores is rarely attempted.

Kennebec River Light Station — Arrowsic

Kennebec River Light Station was built in 1908. Originally called Doubling Point Range Light, it was renamed in 1982. Unattended until 1981, it was maintained by the Squirrel Point Light keeper, who also maintained nearby Doubling Point Light. He moved to Kennebec River Light Station due to the hardship of ferrying his child to school across the ice-choked river in winter.

In 1982, the Coast Guard's first female lighthouse keeper, Karen McLean, took over these lights. She continued to do so until 1987, when her husband, Daniel McLean, replaced her. Kennebec River Light Station is scheduled for automation in 1989.

Characteristics and Location

The Kennebec River Light Station is the only range light in Maine, with an identical two-light system of front and rear wooden towers. When mariners are positioned so the lights are aligned, they know they are in the middle of the channel. The front tower is 18 feet from mean high water to the center of the beacon. The rear tower is 235 yards behind and higher on the shore. It is 33 feet from mean high water to the center of the beacon. The front light is a white beacon with a quick flash; the rear is an equal interval flash every six seconds.

The Kennebec River Light Station is accessible by land and is marked by a sign on Route 127, about 2.7 miles south of Route 1. The unpaved road to the light—still marked Doubling Point Road in places—adds to the confusion about Doubling Point Light and the former Doubling Point Range Light, now called Kennebec River Light Station, where the keeper of all three lights lives (207-442-7811).

Squirrel Point Light, built in 1898 on the southwest corner of Arrowsic, is about three miles farther down Route 127 on Bald Head looking over the Kennebec River to Phippsburg. It has a keeper's dwelling and a white octagonal tower with a walkway. It is 25 feet from mean high water to the center of the beacon—a fixed red light with a white sector visible for ten miles (red) and 13 miles (white). The light and fog signal are operated by radio from the Kennebec River Light Station.

Doubling Point Light is also a white octagonal tower built in 1898 near the upper end of Fiddler Reach, where the Kennebec straightens and heads to Bath. The tower is 23 feet from mean high water to the middle of the beacon—a flashing white light every four seconds, visible for eight miles. This light is also operated by radio from the Kennebec River Light Station.

The tour boat *Argo* out of Boothbay Harbor (207-633-4925 or 207-633-5090) passes Squirrel Point, Doubling Point and Kennebec River lights as well as several other lighthouses in the area.

Seguin Light — Georgetown

Seguin Island is considered one of the most important lighthouse positions on the East Coast and is one of only two lighthouses in New England with a first order lens—the largest beacon. The other first order light marks the entrance to Boston Harbor, at The Graves.

Seguin Light is also the highest on the Maine Coast, not because of the actual tower height but because, like Monhegan Island Light, it was built on high land. Seguin's beacon is 180 feet above mean high water, although the tower itself is only 53 feet high.

Seguin was built in 1795 to mark the mouth of the heavily traveled Kennebec River. It is one of the oldest lighthouses on the Atlantic Coast—the second oldest one in Maine—having been established during the presidency of George Washington.

The salary of Seguin's first keeper ($200 a year) was highly disputed because the government decided there was ample opportunity for him to fish, raise hay for cattle and grow his own produce on the spacious island, and provide firewood for his quarters from the stand of trees that grew there at the time.

In 1936, the Bureau of Lighthouses decided to verify or dispel rumors of a treasure buried on Seguin Island and hired Archie Lane to spend a full year there. He left after nine months, declaring the spot to be free of treasure.

Sequin is one of only a few lighthouses to retain its old lens. At current prices, a new Fresnel lens of equal size would cost $7 million.

Characteristics and Location

Seguin Light is a white cylindrical granite tower connected to the keeper's dwelling on an island two miles south of the mouth of the Kennebec River. The beacon is a fixed white light visible for 18 miles. The station also has a foghorn, among the most powerful on the coast. Frank Bracey, keeper of Seguin from 1926 to 1931, described seagulls flying past being knocked to the ground by the force of the concussion. Seguin holds the highest record for a single year's fog—2734 hours, or 31 percent of the year.

Seguin was attended as a stag light until 1985, when it was automated.

The *Argo* out of Boothbay Harbor (207-633-4925 or 207-633-5090) passes Seguin as well as several other lighthouses in the area.

Hendrick's Head Light — Southport

The first lighthouse on this rocky promontory was erected in 1829 on the west shore of Southport near the mouth of the Sheepscot River. The tower was rebuilt in 1875. Among the fascinating tales of rescue associated with Hendrick's Head is the wreck of a ship from which floated a huge bundle—the only sign of survival in the gale. Inside the bundle, retrieved by the lighthouse keeper from the raging surf, were two feather beds cushioning a box. Inside the box was a baby girl, crying in the freezing cold. The lighthouse keeper and his wife dashed her into their warm kitchen and adopted her as their own when no other survivors were found in the wreck.

Characteristics and Location

Hendrick's Head Light is a white square tower connected to the keeper's dwelling by a covered walkway, reputedly lined with photographs of all of Maine's lighthouses. The bell tower still stands but is not operational, and the dwelling is now privately owned. The tower, 43 feet from mean high water, and 39 feet from the ground to the center of the beacon, has a fixed white light with a red sector visible for 12 miles (white) and nine miles (red). The tour boat *Argo* out of Boothbay Harbor (207-633-4925 or 207-633-5090) passes Hendrick's Head and several other lighthouses in the area.

The Cuckolds — Southport

The Cuckolds Light, about 1000 yards off Cape Newagen at the tip of Southport, tops a barren ledge scoured by heavy seas. It marks two substantial islets upon which many vessels have gone aground as they approached Boothbay Harbor.

In the 1800s, when the harbor was one of the most important on the Maine Coast and hosted an estimated 4000 vessels a year, many requests were made for a fog signal to replace a black wooden tripod that was useful only as a day beacon when there was no fog. The requests were finally granted and the Cuckolds signal house was completed in 1892, with 430 casks of cement, 60,000 bricks, 100 tons of sand, 105 yards of granite masonry, 200 tons of broken stones and pebbles, 70,000 feet of lumber, 3400 pounds of wrought iron work, 4000 pounds of beams and 5900 pounds of columns and railings. The total cost was $24,750, $250 below the appropriated amount.

In 1902, the original hot-air-driven fog signal was replaced by an oil-driven apparatus. Five years later, a lighthouse tower was erected on the roof of the fog signal house, and for the first time the Cuckolds was illuminated.

Characteristics and Location

The Cuckolds Light, 61 feet from mean high water to the center of the beacon, is a group flashing white light every six seconds, visible for 24 miles. Not attended since the 1970s, the light's two-family dwelling has been dismantled by the Coast Guard. The light can be seen just across the channel from Cape Newagen and from aboard the *Argo*, a tour boat out of Boothbay Harbor that passes several lighthouses in the area (207-633-4925 or 207-633-5090).

Ram Island Light — Boothbay

Of Maine's ten Ram Islands, the one off Ocean Point in Boothbay is marked by a lighthouse. Ram Island Light, built in 1883 and joined to the island by a long walkway, is passed often by pleasure boats out of Boothbay Harbor negotiating the scenic Fisherman Island Passage between that island and Ram.

Characteristics and Location

Ram Island Light is a gray tower with a red top on the south side of Fisherman Island Passage at the tip of Linekin Neck. The tower is 36 feet from mean high water to the center of the beacon—a fixed red light with two white sectors, visible for 13 miles. The station also has a foghorn.

Burnt Island Light — Southport

Burnt Island Light, at the entrance to Boothbay Harbor, is one of the most visible to fishermen, landlubbers and recreational boaters. Because of its proximity to the town and its heavy summer traffic, many tourists have visited the light and picnicked there, or simply viewed it from the nearby shore.

Burnt Island Light, built in 1821, is still attended as a family light, and the keeper and his wife can come ashore at will, although not at the same time, to pick up supplies.

The original light at this location was visible to mariners approaching Boothbay Harbor from the southwest just as they cleared the tip of Southport, but not before they gave sufficient berth to The Cuckolds, two ledges lying dead in their path. So in 1888, after several vessels grounded on the rocks, the lantern at Burnt Island was altered to make the light invisible until ships were beyond the offending ledges.

Characteristics and Location

Burnt Island Light (207-633-4841) on the west side of the entrance to Boothbay Harbor, is a white conical tower with a covered way to the keeper's dwelling; it is 61 feet from mean high water to the center of the beacon. The station has a foghorn and a red light with two white sectors flashing every six seconds and visible for 12 miles (red) and 15 miles (white).

Burnt Island Light can be seen from the mainland from the east side of the harbor or from the tour boat *Argo*, which sails from mid-May to mid-October from Fisherman's Wharf past seven lighthouses in the area (207-633-4925 or 207-633-5090).

Bridgton
Otisfield
Long Lake
Pleasant Lake
Casco
Poland Spring
Danville
Upper Gloucester
New Gloucester
Lisbon
Androscoggin
Naples
Peabody Pond
Cook Mills
Webb Mills (Crescent Lake)
N. Pownal
S. Casco
Raymond
Little Sebago Lake
Dry Mills
Gray
Pownal Center
Convene
Sebago
North Sebago
Sebago Lake
267
E. Sebago
North Windham
Freeport
North Yarmouth
West Cumberland
East Baldwin
Steep Falls
Fosters Corner
Cumberland Center
Sebago Lake
Yarmouth
South Windham
West Falmouth
Cumberland Foreside
East Limington
Standish
Little Falls
Falmouth Foreside
Bonny Eagle
Gorham
Portland
Westbrook
Peaks Island
West Buxton
Buxton Center
North Scarborough
Buxton
Hollis Center
Bar Mills
East Waterboro
Salmon Falls
Oak Hill
West Scarborough
Scarborough
Cape Elizabeth
Higgins Beach
Waterboro
Pine Point
Prouts Neck
Goodwins Mills
Saco
Old Orchard Beach
Alfred
Biddeford
Ocean Park
Bay View
Lyman
Camp Ellis
Wood Island
Days Mills
Sanford
Biddeford Pool
Fortunes Rocks
West Kennebunk
Kennebunk
Arundel
Goose Rocks Beach
Cape Porpoise
Kennebunkport
Elms
Kennebunk Beach
Wells
Wells Beach
Moody
Mt. Agamenticus 692
Ogunquit
Cape Neddick
York Beach
Cape Neddick
York Village
York Harbor
Boon Island
Kittery Point
Kittery
Gerrish I.

Southern Coast

Pemaquid Point Light — Bristol

Pemaquid Point Light is one of the most frequently visited and photographed lighthouses on the Maine Coast. It was built in 1827 atop a long picturesque sweep of rocky ledge that juts into the Atlantic from the tip of the Pemaquid peninsula. The surf that pounds the shore here is spectacular.

It became the custom of lighthouse keepers at Pemaquid Point Light to farm in addition to their other chores, and the light's first keeper, Isaac Dunham, built several barns and outbuildings near the site in the ten years he served there.

Characteristics and Location

Pemaquid Point Light is a white pyramidal tower with a dwelling and outbuildings on the west side of the entrance to Muscongus Bay. The tower is 79 feet from mean high water to the center of the beacon—a flashing white light every six seconds, visible for 14 miles.

Photo by Tom Jones

The lighthouse, accessible by land, is about 16.5 miles from Route 1 in Damariscotta, at the end of Route 130. The light is not attended and the old keeper's dwelling is now the Fishermen's Museum, with artifacts and photographs of the lighthouses of the Maine Coast and its fishing industry. Open daily, Memorial Day to Columbus Day, and by appointment; (207-677-2726). Parking for the lighthouse and museum is in the town-owned lot. The rocky ledges around the light attract scores of kite fliers, tide pool explorers, rock scramblers and picnickers. The Pemaquid Art Gallery, Pemaquid Beach Park, Fort William Henry and Colonial Pemaquid are also nearby.

The tour boat *Argo* out of Boothbay Harbor (207-633-4925 or 207-633-5090) passes Pemaquid Point Light as well as several others in the area.

Photo by Bonnie Scott

Monhegan Island Light — Monhegan

As the first land sighted in most trans-Atlantic voyages in the heyday of shipping, Monhegan Island was a prime spot for a lighthouse. One was built on the highest point of land, in almost the center of the island, in 1824, and a fog signal was added in 1854. The foghorn was not effective, however, so far from shore, so a new fog signal was erected on Manana, across the narrow channel from Monhegan. In 1982, the fog station was still attended by up to seven Coast

Guardsmen who maintained a 24-hour watch to send radio beacons and weather reports. The men rowed across to Monhegan to attend that light, which had not had its own keeper since 1959. The old keeper's dwelling was converted to the Monhegan Museum, with exhibits on the geology, fishing and natural history of the island.

Characteristics and Location

Monhegan, site of Maine's first fishing settlement in 1614 and now noted for its resident summer artists and scenic trails, lies nine miles off the the mainland and is accessible year round by the mailboat *Laura B* from Port Clyde (207-372-8848). From mid-June to mid-September the *Balmy Days* out of Boothbay Harbor makes the trip (207-633-2284). There are several seasonal inns and a grocery store, and the Monhegan Museum is open from July through Labor Day.

With Seguin Island, Monhegan was the highest landfall light in Maine, at 178 feet from mean high water to the center of the lens (two feet lower than Seguin). The gray conical tower, 47 feet from the ground to the middle of the lens, has a flashing white light every 30 seconds, visible for 21 miles.

Franklin Island Light — Friendship

When the shipping trade flourished around Friendship and the St. George River in the mid 1800s, many shipwrecks around the shoals and isles of Franklin Island necessitated a better aid to navigation in Muscongus Bay. A light was established on Franklin Island, one of the outer islands of the bay, in 1855, replacing a less effective marker that had been erected there in 1805.

Characteristics and Location

Franklin Island Light is a white tower on the northwest side of Franklin Island with a flashing white light every six seconds, visible for eight miles. The tower is 57 feet from mean high water to the center of the beacon. The keeper's dwelling, formerly attached to the tower, and the outbuildings have been dismantled by the Coast Guard.

The nearest headland, and former mail and supply base, is Friendship.

Photo by Al Kidwell

Marshall Point Light — St. George

Marshall Point Light marks the south entrance to the fishing port of Port Clyde Harbor and the western entrance to Two Bush Channel. The white rubblestone light tower, built in 1823 and refurbished in 1858, has led a comparatively uneventful life in terms of shipwrecks, although the keeper's dwelling, also rubblestone, was so severely struck by lightning in 1895 that it had to be rebuilt. In 1987, the dwelling was leased to the town of St. George.

Characteristics and Location

Marshall Point Light is a white tower on the east side of the south entrance to Port Clyde Harbor. It is 30 feet from mean high water to the center of the beacon—a fixed white light visible for 13 miles. The station also has a foghorn.

The lighthouse is a popular site for artists and photographers. It is accessible by land by following

Route 131 south to Port Clyde, turning left at the main intersection, then turning right immediately beyond the Black Harpoon restaurant onto the paved but unmarked Marshall Point Road. The lighthouse is about .9 mile down this road.

Whitehead Light — St. George

Because Whitehead Light, the principal beacon marking the entrance to the Muscle Ridge Channel, has the highest average fog signal operation in Maine, it has been the scene of much experimentation with fog signaling devices. Among the most unique was a tide-driven fog bell, the first successful attempt to harness the sea for this purpose. It operated in 1838 and 1839 with the rising and falling tide winding a 2000-pound weight-operated spring mechanism that powered the striking mechanism. The tide bell was damaged by the surf and was replaced with a steam whistle like that at West Quoddy Head Light. Diesel engines replaced the steam engines in 1933.

Children of the Whitehead Light keeper at one time attended school in a building close to the station. Since so many families lived on neighboring islands, thirty or more students were in attendance at one time and a hired teacher lived at the keeper's home.

The heroine of Maine lighthouses, Abbie Burgess Grant, daughter of Matinicus Rock lighthouse keeper Samuel Burgess, was appointed assistant keeper at Whitehead when she moved there with her husband, Isaac H. Grant, and their four children in 1875.

The only tarnish on the history of Whitehead Light came in the early 1800s, when lighthouse keeper Ellis Dolph was found to be selling whale oil designated for the beacon to his private customers on the mainland. He was dishonorably discharged after conducting his sideline for two years.

Characteristics and Location

Whitehead Light is a gray tower attached to a red brick service building built in 1807 and rebuilt in 1852 on the west side of the south entrance to Muscle Ridge Channel. The tower is 75 feet from mean high water and 41 feet from the ground to the middle of the beacon—an occulting green light every four seconds, visible for 10 miles. The station still has a foghorn. Formerly a stag light, Whitehead has been unattended since 1972.

Matinicus Rock Light — Matinicus Island

Eighteen miles offshore and 25 miles from the nearest port of Rockland is Matinicus Rock Light, the farthest lighted outpost on the Maine Coast. About halfway between Monhegan and Mount Desert Rock and dead in the track of coasting vessels, Matinicus Rock was an ideal location for a lighthouse. Twin granite lights, one of only two such stations in Maine, were built there in 1848, replacing two wooden towers that survived the lashing of the sea from only 1827 to 1848. The site is continuously scoured by waves that billow to 40 feet and completely engulf the island so that not a blade of grass survives there for long.

Matinicus Rock Light was made famous by Abbie Burgess, the youngest heroine of the Lighthouse Service. When a January 1856 storm kept lighthouse keeper Samuel Burgess on the mainland for four weeks, his 17-year-old daughter Abbie tended the light through the gale and never allowed it to die. The storm—the same one that toppled the Minot's Ledge Light tower in Massachusetts—was so severe that it forced Abbie, her three sisters and her invalid mother into the light tower as waves completely swept 39-acre Matinicus Rock and flooded the keeper's dwelling. Abbie rescued her only pets—four hens—by rushing literally between waves to pluck them from their coop before it was washed away by the storm.

In 1861, Abbie married the son of the new keeper of Matinicus Rock Light, Isaac H. Grant. They had four children there before they were transferred to Whitehead Light in St. George. Abbie was appointed assistant keeper of that light and remained for 15 years until her son took over her post.

Even as a young girl, Abbie kept an especially detailed log of her own, in addition to the keeper's daily log which included every event, wreck and life lost and saved. It may have been due partially to Abbie's well-recorded experiences of her life on the island that the policy of having only one keeper at a lighthouse was changed. For a while, such remote outposts had three keepers on the island simultaneously. However, due to the increasing expense of manning lighthouses, Matinicus Rock Light was automated in 1984.

The light towers at Matinicus Rock have undergone numerous changes, including dismantling of the north tower. Both Matinicus Rock and Cape Elizabeth Light, the only other twin light in Maine, were converted to single lights by government mandate in 1924.

Characteristics and Location

Matinicus Rock Light has a cylindrical gray granite tower and dwelling still attended by the Coast Guard as a stag light. The tower is 90 feet from mean high water, and 48 feet from the ground to the center of the lens, a flashing white light every 10 seconds, visible for 24 miles. The station has a foghorn as well as a radio beacon.

Matinicus Rock, six miles south of Matinicus Island, is home to at least ten species of seabirds including puffins, terns, razorbill auks, shearwaters and petrels, and is the subject of Maine Audubon Society observation cruises which circle the rock in summer (207-781-2330). Captain Richard Moody operates a passenger vessel with trips to Matinicus Rock from Rockland and Matinicus Island. He also passes Owls Head and Rockland Breakwater lights. Call 207-366-3700 or 207-366-3926.

Saddleback Ledge Light — Vinalhaven

When Saddleback Ledge Light was built in 1839, it had the dubious distinction of being the only lighthouse on the East Coast where getting on and off depended on a hoist and boom and bosun's chair. It is the most difficult lighthouse to land at in heavy seas and has not been attended since the 1960s. In calm weather in the old days, however, visitors seemed to have been attracted by the unique style of landing. When W.W. Wells was keeper, he hoisted 42 summer vacationists ashore in a single day.

Saddleback Ledge had a more honorable distinction, however. Even the notoriously critical inspector I.W.P. Lewis could report in 1842 that the lighthouse was the best constructed he had seen and the only one in New England that had been designed by "an architect and engineer."

Saddleback Ledge is one of the three lighthouses on the Maine coast without soil. (The others are Mount Desert Rock and Boon Island off York.) Earth was hauled from the mainland in burlap bags to be tucked into crevices on the ledge so the lighthouse keepers could grow flowers and vegetables. One keeper who managed a few pea vines and hills of potatoes also lovingly tended sprigs of oats that germinated in his compost. Since winter storms swept away whatever soil was brought ashore, however, keepers had to start all over again the following spring.

Saddleback Ledge Light is one of the most isolated outposts on the Maine Coast, sitting almost squarely between Vinalhaven and Isle au Haut at the southern end of Isle au Haut Bay. It was not a favorite assignment among lighthouse keepers, since living there in the 1800s necessitated rowing almost five miles to the nearest mail and supply base of Vinalhaven.

Characteristics and Location

Saddleback Ledge Light is a gray conical tower with a white base 54 feet from mean high water, and 42 feet from the ledge to the middle of the beacon. The white light flashes every six seconds and is visible for 11 miles.

Isle au Haut Light — Isle au Haut

When it was built in 1907, Isle au Haut Light and its fine keeper's dwelling were considered among the most handsome on the Maine coast. But as early as 1934, there was no longer a need for an attended light at this location and the lighthouse property, except for that occupied by the tower, was sold to the highest private bidder. In 1986, the property was purchased by Judi and Jeff Burke, who have transformed the keeper's house into an inn.

Characteristics and Location

The Isle au Haut Light, at the south end of the thoroughfare between Isle au Haut and Kimball Island, is connected to the shore by a wooden bridge. The tower is 48 feet from mean high water to the center of the beacon, which flashes red with a white sector every four seconds and is visible for six miles (red) and eight miles (white). The tower is conical with the lower part built of granite blocks and the upper part of white brick. In 1987, the tower was restored by the Coast Guard.

Isle au Haut is reached by the mail boat from Stonington all year, but more frequently in summer, except Sundays and postal holidays (207-367-5193). The island is the primitive campsite outpost of Acadia National Park, with registration for camping required far in advance. Reservations must be made by mail. For application forms, write to: Acadia National Park, Isle au Haut Reservations, P.O. Box 177, Bar Harbor, Maine 04609. Day visitors can hike the scenic trails and biking is good on the perimeter road which is readily negotiable even on its unpaved stretches. Maps of the island are available in Stonington and at the Acadia National Park visitor center in Bar Harbor.

Photo by Sherman Hasbrouck

Owls Head Light — Owls Head

Owls Head Light stands on a tree-studded promontory jutting into Penobscot Bay below Rockland. The shape which gives the headland its name is readily identified by two hollows in the rocky cliff and a ridge between them which forms the owl's eyes and beak.

In 1826, as Rockland's lime and shipping business began to flourish and schooners bound from Owls Head to Europe frequently wrecked in fog and storms, the numerous petitions to build a lighthouse were granted. Owls Head continued to be an ill-fated location, however. In the 23 years that Joseph Maddocks was keeper, from 1873 to 1896, at least 11 ships were wrecked in the vicinity of the light.

The last keeper of the old Lighthouse Service was Augustus Hamer, who came to Owls Head in 1930. Hamer's Springer Spaniel, Spot, loved to pull on the fog bell rope when ships passed the promontory and then bark as the passing vessels answered with their bells. The dog is credited with guiding the Matinicus mailboat into Rockland by its barking one stormy night. Spot is buried near the foghorn.

Characteristics and Location

Owls Head Light, still attended as a family light (207-594-8960), is a white granite tower 100 feet from mean high water, and 87 feet from the ground to the middle of the beacon—a fixed white light visible for 16 miles. The station also has a foghorn.

The lighthouse is accessible by land and its lovely setting and handsome structure attract many visitors. It is on the National Register of Historic Places and is adjacent to Lighthouse Park, a good picnic spot with fine rocks to scramble on. To reach the light, turn left at Owls Head Post Office, and go downhill towards the harbor. Take the first left and go to the end. Turn left onto the dirt road and continue to open area. The lighthouse is a short walk beyond. Paths to the lower beach are to the left as you leave the parking lot and to the right about 50 feet beyond the gate.

Captain Richard Moody (207-366-3700) has a passenger vessel which passes Owls Head Light on its trips to Matinicus Rock.

While you are in the area, Owls Head Transportation Museum, adjacent to Knox County Airport off Route 73, has exhibits of antique planes and autos, many still in excellent working condition. Open mid-May to mid-October plus designated weekends (207-594-4418).

Rockland Breakwater Light — Rockland

Rockland Breakwater Light was built in 1888 to guide vessels serving Rockland's burgeoning lime shipping industry. The tower is at the end of an almost mile-long breakwater of granite rocks— in itself a landmark familiar to passengers on the ferry to Vinalhaven and to fishermen and pleasure boaters in Rockland Harbor. When a recent proposal to discontinue the light was made known, public outcry kept the tower intact, with the stipulation that the Samoset Resort Hotel, the closest land access, assume responsibility for some of its upkeep. The Coast Guard continues to service the light.

Characteristics and Location

Rockland Breakwater Light is a white square tower

on the corner of a fog signal house at the south end of a 7/8-mile-long breakwater off Jameson's Point. The tower is 39 feet from mean high water to the center of the beacon—a flashing white light every five seconds and visible for 17 miles. The station also has a foghorn.

The light is accessible by land, by following signs from Route 1 to the Samoset Resort Hotel, just north of downtown Rockland, and continuing past the hotel to the end of the road. The breakwater makes a fine hike on a calm day.

The Maine State Ferries to Vinalhaven and North Haven pass this light (207-594-5543).

Photo by Don Marson

Grindle Point Light — Islesboro

The town of Islesboro rescued the Grindle Point Light when it was decommissioned in 1935, and turned the keeper's dwelling into the Sailor's Memorial Museum, which still attracts visitors to its nautical and historical displays.

One of the early lighthouses with a square tower, Grindle Point was built in 1851 at the entrance to Gilkey Harbor, which separates Islesboro from Seven Hundred Acre Island. It is a lovely sheltered anchorage and many pleasure boats moor here. At one point, the lighthouse was abandoned, its beacon replaced by a daymark on a skeleton tower close by; but in 1987 the light was recommissioned.

Characteristics and Location

The lighthouse, on the north side of the entrance to Gilkey Harbor, is 54 feet from mean high water to the center of the beacon, which flashes green every four seconds and is visible for seven miles.

The ferry from Lincolnville Beach to Islesboro (207-789-5611) lands at Grindle Point. The Islesboro Memorial Museum is open from June to September, 10 am to 4 pm, every day except Mondays. This is one of the few lighthouses on islands with overnight accommodations and paved roads. The hills are gentle and the biking is terrific. There is also swimming at Dark Harbor and a public beach at Pendleton Point.

Dice Head Light — Castine

Guarding the mouth of the Penobscot River in Castine since 1937 is the Dice Head Light. A diamond-shaped daymark on a skeleton tower, the light is located near the old lighthouse which is no longer in use. The original lighthouse was built in 1829 but as shipping ebbed in the Penobscot River, the light was no longer attended.

Characteristics and Location

The daymark, on the north side of the entrance to Castine Harbor, is a white beacon flashing every six seconds and is visible for 11 miles. It is 27 feet from mean high water to the center of the light.

Dice Head Light is accessible by land. From Castine continue straight past Fort George about a mile to the end of the road. The old lighthouse is directly ahead and a public path leads down to the daymark at the edge of the water.

Bass Harbor Head Light — Tremont

One of the most scenic lighthouses on the Maine Coast, Bass Harbor Head Light tops a precipitous ledge that drops away into the area on the southwest point of Mount Desert Island. The tower marks the entrance to Blue Hill Bay and Bass Harbor over the Bass Harbor Bar. Built in 1858 opposite the bar, the light was primarily a beacon for coasting ships that often sought refuge from easterly gales in Bass Harbor. The closest fog signals in either direction at the time were at Matinicus Rock and Petit Manan, about 60 miles apart. The tower and adjoining keeper's dwelling still stand in near-original condition.

Photo by Roberta Gray

Characteristics and Location

Bass Harbor Head Light is a white conical tower 56 feet from mean high water to the center of the beacon, an occulting red light flashing every four seconds and visible for 13 miles.

The lighthouse is accessible by land. Follow the paved road where Route 102A bears left just south of Bass Harbor village. There is a parking lot at the lighthouse and, as you face the light, wooden stairs lead from the left to the rocks below. The light is also visible from the Maine State Ferries that leave Bass Harbor for Swans Island and Frenchboro (207-594-5543).

Great Duck Island — Frenchboro

Great Duck Island Light is the only station on the Maine Coast that boasted a schoolhouse for the lighthouse keeper's children. In 1902, the arrival of assistant keeper Nathan Adam Reed, his wife and 16 children swelled the number of children on remote Great Duck Island to 32. A small white school building was erected in 1904 and a teacher was hired. The initial enrollment was 11 pupils. After one of them graduated and continued her education on the mainland, she returned to the lighthouse to instruct her brothers and sisters.

Great Duck Island was named for a pond that once filled a depression in the center of the island, where huge flocks of ducks came every spring to raise their young.

In 1890, in the heyday of commerce, the lighthouse and fog signal were erected on the island to direct coasting vessels into Bass Harbor and Southwest Harbor, both frequently used for refuge in a storm. Behind the lighthouse, the homes of the three keepers were built side by side. A small burial ground surrounded by a white fence marks the grave of two shipwrecked mariners who were found frozen to death in each others arms and were buried in a shallow grave because the ground was frozen and rowing to the mainland in the middle of winter was impossible. When the weather softened and the families visited the burial site, they decided to let it remain, and every Memorial Day a brief service was held and flowers were placed on the grave. On the north end of the island was a small cottage frequently occupied by fishermen and families who raised sheep. At one time, 500 sheep were raised on the island and roamed freely in the fields and woods.

Characteristics and Location

Duck Island Light is a white cylindrical tower 67 feet from mean high water, and 42 feet from the ground to the middle of the beacon. The light flashes red every 5 seconds and is visible for 19 miles. The station also has a radio beacon. The light was automated in 1986.

The nearest headland is Bass Harbor, about 7 miles northwest.

Bear Island Light — Cranberry Isles

At the entrance to Northeast Harbor, on one of the highest points of land on Bear Island looking out to sea over the Cranberry Isles, is Bear Island Light, a white tower rising 100 feet above mean high water. Built in 1839 and rebuilt in 1889, the lighthouse complex was also a buoy depot, where several attendants cleaned and painted navigational aids so they would be in good repair when they were needed. The light was also outfitted with a coaling station, so buoy tenders could refuel while downeast.

Characteristics and Location

Bear Island Light used to be attended and had a flashing beacon visible for 17 miles, but in 1982 it was deactivated and replaced with lighted buoys. Ownership of the lighthouse was transferred to Acadia National Park in 1987. The best view of the tower is from the Beal and Bunker mailboat *Sea Queen* which passes close to Bear Island on its trip from the Northeast Harbor Town Pier to Cranberry Isles and Sutton Island (207-244-3575).

The Frenchman's Bay Boating Company also comes close to Bear Island on its trip from Bar Harbor to Seal Harbor during July and August. Call 207-288-3322 or write Bob Collier, P.O. Box 88, Bar Harbor, Maine 04609.

Baker Island Light — Cranberry Isles

Baker Island Light, a well-known landmark near the entrance to Frenchman's Bay, marks the treacherous shoals around the Cranberry Isles. It is primarily a harbor entrance light, situated on 123-acre Baker Island, where former keepers raised cattle.

The light's first keeper was long-time island resident William Gilley, who stayed on Baker Island an additional 21 years to attend the beacon. There are tremendous views from the top of the tower, which is 105 feet above mean high water, and the site has always been frequently visited by Mount Desert Island summer folk.

Characteristics and Location

Built in 1828 and rebuilt in 1855, Baker Island Light is a white stone tower 43 feet from the ground to the middle of the lens with a white flashing light every 10 seconds. The beacon, southwest of the entrance to Frenchman's Bay, is visible for 10 miles. The lighthouse is no longer attended.

Egg Rock Light — Winter Harbor

Egg Rock Light, marking the entrance to Frenchman's Bay, is one of the foggiest and most exposed locations on the Maine Coast. The gale of March 21, 1876 moved the bell tower 30 feet, and it was again damaged in the gale of December 28, 1887. To avoid future calamity, a new bell tower was built in skeleton fashion and bolted to the ledge. The boathouse, by necessity at the water's edge, has been carried out to sea more than once.

Since Egg Rock has been modernized by the Coast Guard, it has become known as the most homely lighthouse on the Maine Coast.

At unattended stations the Coast Guard had been replacing the old labor-intensive Fresnel lenses with airway beacons because the beacons required less maintenance. When it replaced the Fresnel lens and protective glass lantern at Egg Rock, it lopped off the top of the platform which supported them and erected back-to-back airway beacons. Public criticism caused the Coast Guard to install a protective cupola in 1986 to improve the light's appearance. On some subsequent lens replacements the original glass lantern has been retained to conceal the modern beacons.

Characteristics and Location

Egg Rock Light, a white square tower 64 feet from mean high water, and 40 feet from the ground to the center of the beacon, has a foghorn and a red light flashing every five seconds, visible for 13 miles. The Frenchman's Bay Boating Company makes three trips a day from Bar Harbor past Egg Rock Light between Memorial Day and Columbus Day weekend. Call 207-288-3322 or write Bob Collier, P.O. Box 88, Bar Harbor, Maine 04609.

Mount Desert Rock Light — Mount Desert Island

Mount Desert Rock Light, 20 miles south of the closest harbor on Mount Desert Island, is one of the most isolated and exposed stations on the Atlantic Coast. Although Boon Island is considered remote, it is only nine miles from shore, and the outpost at Matinicus Rock is just six miles from Matinicus Island.

Mount Desert Rock Light is also one of the Coast's most inhospitable sites. Lighthouse keepers have attempted to grow flowers and vegetables there since the station was built in 1830 by hauling burlap bags full of soil from the mainland every spring to tuck into crevices in the otherwise barren ledge. By fall's end, however, the soil had been washed away by the storms that scour what has become known as "God's Rock Garden." It is no wonder. Lighthouse records show that a 57-ton stone, six feet thick, 18 feet long and 14 feet wide, was relocated by the waves in 1842.

Characteristics and Location

Mount Desert Rock Light is a gray granite conical tower 75 feet from mean high water, and 58 feet from the ground to the middle of the beacon—a flashing white light every 15 seconds, visible for 24 miles. The station, which is no longer attended, also has a foghorn.

Petit Manan Light — Milbridge

Petit Manan Light was built in 1817 at one of the foggiest locations on the eastern seaboard. In a 31-year period, the foghorn operated at an annual average of 1691 hours, or about 19 percent of the year.

Standing 123 feet above mean high water, Petit Manan is the second tallest light on the Maine Coast. (Boon Island off York is 133 feet above mean high water.) Old timers like to say the light was built twice. After the granite was cut and assembled at a quarry in Trenton, the stones were numbered, dismantled and later reassembled on Petit Manan.

The tower was threatened by a chain of gales that swept Petit Manan in 1886 and caused the top of the tower, which had been loosened by the great storm of 1856, to begin to break away from the rest of the granite structure. Winter winds of that year swayed the entire upper section back and forth to such an alarming degree that the lighthouse was extensively reinforced the following summer. Had repairs been procrastinated, the December gale of 1887 would most certainly have toppled the tower.

Although the lighthouse is only about two miles from the headland at Petit Manan Point, its mailing base was Milbridge and during a hard winter in the old days the lighthouse keepers did not receive their mail for months at a time, since the ice buildup on their boat slip made launching their small craft impossible. Even telephone communication was not reliable to alleviate their isolation, since severe storms often swept away the cable until spring, when the cable boat was able to make repairs. So radio communication became essential, especially during shipwrecks, for the keepers to radio for help from the mainland when they could not launch a rescue boat from the lighthouse station.

Characteristics and Location

Petit Manan is a gray granite tower 123 feet from mean high water, and 119 feet from the ground to the middle of the beacon, on the east point of Petit Manan Island south of Milbridge. The beacon flashes white every 10 seconds and is visible for 26 miles. Petit Manan's old second order light is on prominent display at the Shore Village Museum in Rockland (207-594-4950). The light is more than 20 feet high when fully assembled. Another Petit Manan artifact at this fascinating museum, and one that indicates the degree of workmanship even at remote outposts, is a brass gargoyle from the end of the rain downspout of the keeper's dwelling. Petit Manan's fog signal was powered by steam, and the water for the steam engine came from rain funneled from the roof into wooden tanks in the basement of the dwelling.

Captain Barna Norton of Jonesport (207-497-5933) provides transportation to Petit Manan and six other nearby islands and their lighthouses.

Nash Island Light — Addison

Nash Island Light was built in 1838 at the entrance to Pleasant and Harrington bays off Cape Split. The site marks very shoaly water in the path from Petit Manan into Moosabec Reach.

Nash Island is one of the few outposts where the children of the lighthouse keepers attended school on the island. When Captain John Purrington arrived with his large family in the 1930s, part of the keeper's dwelling was outfitted as a schoolroom and a teacher was hired from the mainland. The children boarded on the mainland and attended Jonesport High School in the higher grades, however, and after graduation they became fishermen, continuing the close contact with the sea.

Characteristics and Location

Nash Island Light is a white square tower off the east side of the mouth of Pleasant Bay. The beacon has been discontinued and replaced by a buoy, but the tower still remains, 51 feet from mean high water to the center of the lantern. It is slated for eventual dismantling, however.

Captain Barna Norton of Jonesport (207-497-5933) charters his boat to Nash Island as well as six other lighthouses in the vicinity.

Moose Peak Light — Jonesport

Moose Peak Light, on the east point of Mistake Island and east of Great Wass Island, rivals Seguin and Whitehead lights for being the foggiest location on the Maine Coast. The thick fog that rolls out of the Bay of Fundy and blankets this island caused the fog signal at Moose Peak to operate for 181 consecutive hours in 1916.

Characteristics and Location

Moose Peak Light, built in 1827 and rebuilt in 1887, is a white tower 72 feet from mean high water, and 57 feet from the ground to the center of the beacon. It flashes white every 30 seconds and is visible for 26 miles. The station's foghorn is still operating.

Captain Barna Norton (207-497-5933) provides transportation to Moose Peak Light as well as six others in the vicinity.

Libby Island Light — Machiasport

Known for years as Machias Light, Libby Island Light was erected in 1817 at the entrance to Machias Bay. One of the earliest light stations on the Maine Coast, the original tower still stands, although the outbuildings and dwellings of the three keepers have been dismantled.

Libby Island Light marks the two Libby Islands which ships first encounter when entering the channel into Machias Bay. In spite of the strong beacon, the islands remained a hazard to shipping; 35 vessels were wrecked at this outpost in the last half of the 19th century and 15 seamen were killed. Among the dangers was fog; in warm weather especially thick fog banks from the Bay of Fundy moved in rapidly. The other hazard was the sandbar that joined the Libby Islands; it was invisible at high water but large vessels could not clear it. Among the wrecks on Libby Islands were the schooner *Caledonia* out of Nova Scotia in 1878. The captain mistook the passage between the Libby Islands for another in the area that was more negotiable.

The history of the light is also laced with a chain of narrow escapes and drownings among the keepers, as in the summer of 1918 when two keepers were fishing just offshore and approached too near a breaker. Their boat capsized and the keeper, who could not swim, drowned.

Characteristics and Location

Libby Island Light is a conical granite tower on the southernmost of the Libby Islands. The beacon, visible for 25 miles, is a white group light flashing every 20 seconds atop a tower 91 feet from mean high water, and 42 feet from the ground to the center of the lens. The station also has a foghorn.

Captain Barna Norton of Jonesport (207-497-5933) provides transportation to Libby Island Light and five other lighthouses in the vicinity, including Machias Seal Island Light, home to puffins, storm petrels, razorbill auks and terns.

West Quoddy Head Light — Lubec (Cover Photo)

West Quoddy Head is Maine's famous red and white striped lighthouse looking high over the Bay of Fundy from the easternmost point of land in the U.S. The lighthouse was built in 1808, rebuilt in 1858 and outfitted with a steam whistle—the most powerful fog signal known at that time—in 1869. The blast sounded like that from a steam locomotive. Before the steam whistle, the tower had a bell which had to be hand struck in thick weather. In 1827, the lighthouse keeper at West Quoddy Head was allotted an extra $60 annually for time spent ringing the bell.

Characteristics and Location

West Quoddy Head Light, in Quoddy Head State Park, marks the southwest side of the entrance to Quoddy Roads channel. The light tower is 83 feet from mean high water and 49 feet from the ground to the middle of the beacon. The white group light, which flashes every 15 seconds, is visible for 18 miles. The station still has a powerful foghorn.

Although West Quoddy Head Light is currently attended by the Coast Guard as a family light (207-733-2107), automation is planned for 1988. The state park, with picnic tables and fireplaces, is open free from May 30 to Labor Day and weekends until November 1. The park has a nature trail along the high shore with railings separating the path from the steep drop. There are spectacular views over the surf and Grand Manan Island can be seen to the south.

Index

Brooks
Freedom
Knox Center
Sandy Pond
Frye Mtn. 1140
Center Montville
Morrill
Waldo
Swanville
Mt. Waldo
Prospect
Searsport
City Point
Belfast
North Searsmont
Liberty
Belmont Corner
Searsmont
East Northport
Bayside
Northport
Dice Head
Pripet
Harborside
Cape R
Islesboro
Sheepscot Pond
Lincolnville Center
Appleton
Ducktrap
Lincolnville
Mt. Megunticook 1385
Dark Harbor
ISLESBORO
Washington
Hope
Stickney Corner
South Hope
Grindle Point
Union
East Union
Camden
North Waldoboro
West Rockport
Rockport
Pulpit Harbor
Rockland Breakwater
North Haven
Warren
Rockland
Waldoboro
Thomaston
Owls Head
South Warren
Ash Point
South Thomaston
Vinalhaven
Hurricane I.
Broad Cove
Cushing
Bremen
St. George
Sprucehead
Medomak
Long Cove
Friendship
Mid Coa
Pleasant Point
Tenants Harbor
Martinsville
Whitehead
Louds I.
Port Clyde
Mosquito I.
Muscongus Bay
Marshall Point
Georges Islands
Metinic Island
Matinicus
Matinicus Island
Franklin Island
Ragged Island
Criehaven
Matinicus Rock
Monhegan Island
Monhegan
Harrington
Addison
Columbia
Indian River
Cherryfield
Unionville
Milbridge
Smithville
West Jonesport
Sullivan
Wyman
South Addison
Ashville
Steuben
Gouldsboro
West Gouldsboro
Nash Island
South Gouldsboro
Prospect Harbor
Bois Bubert I.
Winter Harbor
Corea
Petit Manan Point
Petit Mana

Ellsworth
Surry
Trenton
West Trenton
Lamoine
East Lamoine
Marlboro
Lamoine Beach
Hancock
Hancock Point
West Sullivan
Sullivan
Sorrento
Egg Rock
Hulls Cove
Bar Harbor
Penobscot
South Penobscot
North Penobscot
Blue Hill
East Blue Hill
Blue Hill Falls
Newbury Neck
Union River Bay
Western Bay
Somesville
Cadillac Mtn. 1530
Otter Creek
Bear Island
Bartlett I.
Long I.
MT DESERT ISLAND
Seal Cove
West Tremont
Southwest Harbor
Tremont
Northeast Harbor
Islesford
Mansel
Cranberry Isles
Bernard
Bass Harbor
Bass Harbor Head
Baker I.
Baker Island
Great Gott I.
West Brooksville
North Brooksville
South Brooksville
Brooksville
Sedgwick
Sargentville
Haven
Brooklin
Naskeag
Blue Hill Bay
DEER ISLE
Deer Isle
Sunset
Sunshine
Oceanville
Stonington
Atlantic
Black I.
SWANS ISLAND
Minturn
Swans Island
Great Duck I.
Great Duck Island
Frenchboro
Long Island
Marshall I.
Isle au Haut
Lookout
Isle au Haut Bay
ISLE AU HAUT
Mount Desert Rock
Eastport
North Lubec
Lubec
West Lubec
Whiting
Rocky Lake
Gardner Lake
West Quoddy Head
South Trescott
Eastern Head
Jacksonville
Machias
East Machias
East Stream
Machiasport
Kennebec
North Cutler
Cutler
Western Head
Bucks Harbor
Starboard
Gross I.
Libby I.
Libby Island
Roque Island
Head Harbor I.
Moose Peak
Northern Coast